Restoring
RELATIONSHIPS
with Your
PARENTS

JIM WILSON

Published by Community Christian Ministries
P.O. Box 9754, Moscow, Idaho 83843
208.883.0997 | www.ccmbooks.org

Jim Wilson, *Restoring Relationships with Your Parents*
Copyright © 2026 by Community Christian Ministries.

Cover by Samuel Dickison.
Interior design by Valerie Anne Bost.

Printed in the United States of America.

26 27 28 29 30 31 32 33 34 35   10 9 8 7 6 5 4 3 2 1

Honor your father and your mother, so that
you may live long in the land the Lord your
God is giving you. (Exod. 20:12)

OUR COUNTRY IS FULL of broken families. Whether you are a Christian or not, from a broken family or a whole one, God calls you to honor your parents. The apostle Paul tells us this "is the first commandment with a promise—'so that it may go well with you and that you may enjoy long life on the earth'" (Eph. 6:2-3).

Your relationship with your parents affects your relationships with your spouse and children. If you are not yet married, a good way to prepare for those future relationships is to reestablish a good relationship with your parents.

The Ten Commandments give us two statements that relate to this. The first is the Exodus quote above. Here is the second:

> You shall not make for yourself an idol in the form of anything in heaven above or on the earth beneath or in the waters below. You shall not bow down to them or worship them; for I, the Lord your God, am a jealous God, punishing the children for the sin of the fathers to the third and fourth generation of those who hate me, but showing love to thousands who love me and keep my commandments. (Deut. 5:8–10)

God says that He will punish children for the sins of the fathers to the third and fourth generation. This has stumbled and troubled people for a long time. How can a just God punish you for someone else's sin? The answer is that He does not.

> Yet you ask, "Why does the son not share the guilt of his father?" Since the son has done what

is just and right and has been careful to keep all my decrees, he will surely live. The soul who sins is the one who will die. The son will not share the guilt of the father, nor will the father share the guilt of the son. The righteousness of the righteous man will be credited to him, and the wickedness of the wicked will be charged against him. (Ezek. 18:19–20)

God does not hold great-grandchildren responsible for what great-grandfather did. Ezekiel says very clearly, "The soul who sins shall die" (v. 20, NKJV). The person who is in sin is the one who will be held accountable.

What the Deuteronomy passage *is* saying is that sin flows downhill—and it does so for three and four generations. Look at your parents and grandparents. Can you see how you are affected by the things your parents did, and how they were affected by your grandparents? The sinful influence of our ancestors affects us. This is generational bad news.

However, the sentence in Deuteronomy does not end with verse 9—it continues with something more wonderful. "But showing love to thousands who love me and keep my commandments" (Deut. 5:10). God punishes the children for three and four generations, but He shows love to *thousands*—not just thousands of people, but *thousands of generations*. "Know therefore that the Lord your God is God; he is the faithful God, keeping his covenant of love to *a thousand generations* of those who love him and keep his commandments" (Deut. 7:9). Sin and hatred of God cause downward movement to three or four generations, and obedience and love of God cause upward movement to a thousand generations.

How do we turn our lives from three and four generations going downhill to a thousand generations going uphill? If you are part of a broken family, the solution seems obvious: get converted, leave home, and marry a Christian. That should turn it around, because you are not going to do life the way your parents did, right? You are going to love God and keep His commandments.

Certainly, a major part of the solution is to become a Christian, keep God's commandments, and marry a Christian who also keeps His commandments. You *must* do those things. Without them, you can expect more bad generations.

However, although these actions are a very important part of the generational turnaround, they alone bring no automatic guarantee of halting the curse. We still have the descending promise of three and four generations, and leaving to establish a new home does not change that. Even if you have no contact with your parents, you carry those relationships and the effects of them with you into your marriage. I have heard this many times: "I decided I was not going to be the kind of father (or mother) who raised me. I would become a Christian, marry a Christian, and do it right. I became a Christian, married a Christian, and I am doing it wrong, just like my parents."

Leaving your parents is not the answer. What you need to do is to *reestablish relationships with your parents*. When you get married, you will have children, and those children are going to need grandparents. If you are estranged from your parents, your children will be deprived of a very important part of their growth. They need grandparents; they need aunts and uncles; they need cousins. The entire family is important. In fact, the family is *more* important than the church. God created the family first. Of course, the best family is a Christian family, but your own extended family is what God speaks of and gives examples of in the Scripture.

My family holds regular reunions. The year my mother was eighty-four, her six sons, their wives, their children, and their grandchildren all met for a reunion in Moscow, Idaho. To see how all the children and grandchildren got along with each other was great. It was a wonderful time, and it was very important. Every family needs this.

If you are in the second or third bad-news generation, you do not have to wait through more bad generations. It is possible to turn the descent around now. But unless you change your relationship with your parents and grandparents, you will have to wait two more generations. (And preaching the gospel to your parents does not change the relationship. It needs to be repaired first.)

About 400 years before Christ, the prophet Malachi gave a negative conditional prophecy: "See, I will send you the prophet Elijah before the great and dreadful day of the Lord comes. He will turn the hearts of the fathers to their children, and the hearts of the children to their fathers; or else I will come and strike the land with a curse" (Mal. 4:5-6).

The angel Gabriel alludes to this prophecy in Luke 1:17: "And he [John] will go on before the Lord, in the spirit and power of Elijah, to turn the hearts of the fathers to their children and the disobedient to the wisdom of the righteous, to make ready a people prepared for the Lord."

Notice that to stop the curse from happening, hearts must be turned both ways.[1] Unless you do this, you are asking for another generation of bad news. You cannot expect to be a good husband or a good father, a good wife or a good mother, if you have not turned your heart to your own father and mother.

Because we have not obeyed God's command to honor our parents, we may be in the third- and fourth-generation promise, and we will not live long on the earth (cf. Eph. 6:3). The land is in danger of being smitten with a curse. The Malachi text is a call to repentance, a turn-around of the heart.

We can turn our family around by obeying what the Ten Commandments tell us: *Honor your father and your mother* (Exod. 20:12). We are promised that a thousand generations of blessing come from keeping God's commandments, and this is one of them. If you want to turn the flow around, this is primary.

How do you honor parents who are not honorable? You may have parents who are divorced. You may have a father who left home before you were born, and you don't even know him. You try to get in touch with him, and he does

1. Although most of my illustrations in this context are speaking to children, this is even more important for parents. If you are a Christian parent reading this, turn your heart toward your own parents, and turn your heart toward your children.

not want to know you. How do you honor someone you don't know? How do you honor someone who is an alcoholic, mistreats his wife, or mistreats his children?

The Scripture says to honor your father and mother because they are your father and mother, *not* because they are honorable. When God tells us to love our enemies, does He mean that our enemy is lovely? Does he have to *deserve* love? No. Love is based upon the person who does the loving. Likewise, honor has to do with the person doing the honoring, not the person being honored.

Do you know any children who have been mistreated at home? How do they act in school? Poorly. On the other hand, if children are treated with respect at home, how do they act in school? Generally, they do well. If you want to make someone *unrespectable*, treat them with no respect. The opposite is true as well. Just as love makes people lovely, respect causes them to be respectable. As Christians, we do not honor, love, and respect people because they deserve it; we do it because they *need* it. Fathers and mothers need it. "No, they've got to earn my respect first." No, they don't. If you want to turn your family around, then *you* obey God's command: honor your father and your mother. If you have not honored them, confess that as sin first and then choose to honor them.

Here are some suggestions for how to go about either reestablishing relationships with your parents or making them better.

First, write two letters home. Do not write, "Dear Mom and Dad." If you write that, who answers the letter? Mom. Dads are illiterate when it comes to answering letters. In many cases, the father thinks that any communication is between mom and the kids. He doesn't think *he* ever gets a letter, even if it is addressed to both Mom and Dad. So, write a letter to your father and a separate one to your mother. Make them very clearly separate. Put on the outside "Dad Only," "Mom Only." (Yes, I am suggesting sending actual letters in the mail. It will mean more than an email.)

When you write to your father, include at least five things.[2] I recommend covering one element per paragraph as follows:

1. **TELL YOUR FATHER HOW MUCH YOU RESPECT HIM.** If you do not respect him, do not write the letter until you do respect him. You must not

2. If you have previously been rebellious towards your parents, there is one more element you should add at the beginning of your letters. First, you must confess to God your rebellion to your father or mother, and now also confess it to your earthly father in this letter, with no excuses or accusations.

be hypocritical. But not respecting your father is not one of your options. How can you do it?

First, confess this disrespect for your father to God. Your father is to be honored because he is your father. God has commanded you to honor him. It is not optional. If you do not honor him, then you have sinned. The same is true with your mother. Sin is forgivable, and repentance is required.

Now with freedom and sincerity, write to your father how much you respect him. If he is not respectable, make sure you are not being dishonest. It would be a lie if you said, "I respect you for divorcing Mom, for being a drunk, for . . ." No. Don't respect him for anything other than being your father. "I respect you as my father."

2. TELL HIM HOW MUCH YOU LOVE HIM. If you do not love him, that has to be corrected first. You might object that you would have loved him if he had loved you first, but he didn't. I'm sure that is true, and he *should* have loved you first. As a father, he should have loved you so that your natural response would have been a loving one. But we cannot go back to childhood and start over. Even if we could, that does not guarantee that your father would do it any different the second time. We address the problem from where we are, not from where we should be.

One of the reasons your father didn't love you may be because *he* had never been loved. You are turning that around.

If you had to answer for your father, would he say that his father loved him? I have asked many college students this over the years. The answer I usually get is, "No, his dad didn't love him. He's told me all the fights they had."

Next, would he say that his wife loves him? No, mom doesn't love him. Would he say that his children love him? No, he doesn't think his kids love him. Would he say that God loves him? He doesn't know God; he's not a Christian.

Do you mean to tell me that your father doesn't think God loves him, his father loved him, his wife loves him, or his children love him? And you wonder why he drinks too much! He sees that everyone who should be close to him does not love him.

"His perception is wrong. We *do* love him, and God loves him."

That's not what I asked. Does he *think* that you all love him? No.[3]

---

3. Of course, sometimes the people I speak with acknowledge that they don't love their father and that their mother hates him.

So here we have a person who *couldn't* love you first because he has never been loved. He doesn't know *how* to love.

I used to ask this question when speaking to a crowd: "How many of you know that your parents love you?" Ninety-five percent would raise their hand.

Then I would ask, "How many of you think they expressed it to you adequately?" Only half of those hands would stay up.

"Of those who think it was expressed adequately, how many could have used more love?" Everybody's hands stayed up. *Nobody* gets enough love at home, even when love is there.

You are now an adult, and as a Christian you have unlimited access to love and forgiveness—a love that your family does not have if they are not Christians. If you are waiting for them to love you first, you've got it all backwards. *You* are now the source of love for your family. You are the vehicle to love your parents. Straighten out your unlove for them with God. As a Christian, confess this lack of love to Him. Is it sin? Yes, it is sin. It is disobedience to the command of God. We have been commanded to love our neighbors, love the brothers, and love our enemies. Your father fits into one of those categories. Confess this lack of love and forsake it. After you have confessed and have been forgiven, choose to love your father.[4] This love requires expression, so tell him in this paragraph.

3. TELL YOUR FATHER HOW GRATEFUL YOU ARE TO HIM. You may be grateful for a lot of things. Enumerate them. Or you might have to go back to pre-school days to think of something. Think of it and thank him. Go back to some nostalgia; tell him how much you appreciated sitting on his lap when you were three, or the fishing trip you had that one time. If you are not grateful, then as with respect and love, it is your problem, not his. The procedure is the same. Confess your unthankfulness to God. When you are forgiven, express your thankfulness to your father.

After I had been teaching this for years, I wrote a letter to my mother. (My father had already passed away.) Most of it was just news, but I put one last sentence in of gratefulness and praise to her, and she called on the telephone to talk to me about it. Nobody gets enough! Start expressing respect, love, and thankfulness.

---

4. The confession must be done first—you cannot obey on top of accumulated disobedience. Once you are clean, you can choose to obey this command, with God's help.

These elements are necessary and required. The next two are suggestions for further ways to convey respect.

4. ASK YOUR FATHER FOR HIS AUTO-BIOGRAPHY. He probably won't write one, but he will be glad that you want to know about him. If you live near your parents, you can ask your dad for this in person. One young woman told me she couldn't write home because her parents lived in the same town. I told her to just ask him. So she asked her father for his autobiography, and this man who is normally extremely quiet talked for four hours. She asked, and he was so glad to be asked.

5. ASK YOUR FATHER FOR ADVICE, IN GENERAL AND ON SPECIFIC MATTERS. This is part of honor. Has he given you advice before, and you didn't like it? Unsolicited advice is generally much rougher than requested advice. It is rougher on you because you didn't want it, and it is *given* rougher because you didn't want it. But when you request advice, the person is usually much more considerate, much more thoughtful, and the advice will be better.

Ask for counsel, and be open to it. You might be really surprised at the advice you get. There are very few parents who are not concerned about the direction their children go and what they do. When you ask, you might find that they were just waiting to be asked, and they will be considerate.

If you are still single, this is especially true regarding anyone you are dating. Ask your father what he thinks of this guy/girl. You may hear things you don't want to hear. When you do, you had better listen. Even if your father is not a Christian, he's been around a while. His answers may be sheer prejudice, but likely they are not. He knows you, and he knows people, so pay attention. If he dislikes the person you are going with, go slow. Even if this man or woman is absolutely right for you and you both know it, it is not right until your parents *also* know it. It is wise to go slow even if you are right and they are wrong.

Some parents will say it doesn't make any difference to them what you do, and you should just do what you want. Don't believe them! They think that is the proper thing to say because you are an adult. Ask them, "*If* you were going to give me advice, what would you want me to do?" If they still don't give you advice, but you know your parents well enough to figure out what they think, pay attention to that, even if they are not willing to tell you outright.

* * *

Your father may not answer the letter you have written him, but he will almost certainly read it more than once, and he will not throw it away. If you have Christian siblings, tell them what you are doing and encourage them to do the same thing.

Next, write the same kind of letter to your mother, but with one change. The first paragraph should express your love to her, and the second paragraph should communicate your respect. Both sexes of the human race need love and respect from both sexes. But of the two, women need love more than they need respect, and men need respect more than they need love. Tell your mother how much you love her; then tell her how much you respect her. The rest of the letter can follow the same pattern as the letter to your father.

As much as possible, follow up on the letters by *spending time with your parents.* Show them with your attention that they are valuable to you. When you go home, express affection to your parents physically. Don't do the polite hug. Get into it. Really give them a squeeze. Maybe even a kiss! Just rock the old man. Surprise your mom.

You may receive a favorable response to your letters. If you do not receive a response, do not think that you did something wrong. Be patient and keep on giving. Some cultures (e.g. those of Northern Europe) are not expressive with their emotions, except for lost tempers. This kind of expression from you may be embarrassing for your parents. But they still want and need to receive this expressed love, even if they do not know how to return it.

If your parents are still alive, it's not too late to do this. One man I know who is in his late fifties wrote this kind of letter to his father. His mother replied, "I have been married to your father for sixty years. When he read your letter, that was the first time in our marriage I saw tears in his eyes."

Some years ago, my wife Bessie and I held a summer school of practical Christianity at the Delta House of the University of Idaho. Respect for parents was one of the subjects. About forty students attended. Because the class was big, I did not get to know everyone well and did not know the effect of the teaching.

The following fall, at a noon Bible study at nearby Washington State University, I was teaching the same subject again, and one of the students spoke up. "I heard this at the Delta House last summer, and I took action," he said. "When I was sixteen, my father kicked me out of the house and told me he would never see me again. Later, I became a Christian and married a Christian woman, and now I am a graduate student in economics. I had never seen my father since he kicked me out of the house. This summer, I wrote two letters, one to my father, and one to my mother. I didn't know it, but my parents were on the brink of divorce, living in separate bedrooms at home in North Dakota.

"It took me several days to write each letter, so I sent them a few days apart—but for some reason, the letters arrived on the same day, and both my parents were home when the mail came. Seeing that the letters were addressed separately, my mother took her letter to her room, and my father took his letter to his room. After reading them, they came out and traded letters, and went back to their rooms to read the other letter. When they came out the second time, my father had tears in his eyes. He told my mother, 'I'm flying out to Pullman to see my son.'"

He had seen his father between the summer school and the fall Bible study. It saved his parents' marriage.

Another student who had recently graduated told me of the awful relationship he had with his father, and I made this suggestion of writing letters. Some months later, when I was speaking to another group on this subject, he spoke up. "Jim told me to do this several months ago, but I wasn't going to. I *hated* my father. In fact, one day I was going to write to tell him what I really thought of him and what a lousy father he had been. I had the entire letter in my head. But when I sat down to write, instead of that letter, I wrote the kind that Jim told me. My father got the letter, and he came down from Spokane immediately to see me. He's dying now, and I read the Scripture to him by his bedside." It reestablished the relationship.

If you already have a good relationship with your parents, go ahead and write these letters anyway. It won't hurt. One young man I know did this, and a few weeks later, he told me he had gotten a letter back from his dad. I asked him what it said. "My father said that he wrote a letter like this to *his* father when he was my age, and, boy, was it good to get one from me!" That is your thousand generations, when you do it right.

What do you do with disappointment? Another student wrote two letters to her mom, the first about the love and respect, and a second one later asking for advice. The mother's response to the first letter was, "Why are you being so soupy?" and the second reply was in anger: "Why do you need this information?"

You can expect questions like this the first time around—so send more than one letter. Likewise, if you come from a family that never hugs, the first time you hug your father, he'll stand there like a fencepost. It will be awkward. *Keep doing it.* Hug him when you get home, but also, when you're at home, hug him every time he walks by.[5]

This might make him ask, "What's your angle?" or "What is this going to cost me?"

Say, "Dad, do you really want to know? If you buy me lunch, I'll tell you." Get together with him. Rather than being disappointed at his response, consider those questions an opportunity to do more.

Tell him, "Dad, here is why I'm doing this. I know you love me very much, but I have had to take it by faith. You

---

5. How can a child show physical affection to a father who has abused him/her? Suppose you were molested by your father, and you are not up to hugging him because he does not respond like a father. In this case, I do not suggest that you hug him. Express your love some other way that is not physical. Do you not love him? Again, take care of that. Confess it and choose to love your father. Then find a different form of expression for his benefit and your benefit.

A few decades ago, a young woman with this background attended our School of Practical Christianity. It was so clear that she needed a father. Her father was from another country, and he lived overseas. I suggested that she write to him and say, "Dad, I need a father. I need to be hugged; I need to hug you. Dad, will you be my father?" He wrote back a repentant, broken-down letter saying, "Yes, I'll be your father." She needed a father, and he needed to *be* one. Their reconciliation was based upon her giving him respect. I cannot guarantee that a reconciliation will happen in every instance; nevertheless, it is very important that you respect and love and be grateful to your parents, however they might respond.

have not been the best expresser of your love. So, growing up I did not think you loved me. You fed me and clothed me and housed me and sent me off to school. I know that is love, but there's more to love than that, and I have needed more. You wondered why I got in trouble in high school and college. It's because I needed more affection than you were giving me. I was boy crazy because I was looking for the male affection I was missing at home. I don't think you would want me to get it somewhere else now. I still need my father, and you need me, so I thought I'd come home and prime the pump."

Here is a very important caveat: if you tell your parents that you are giving them affection because you did not get enough growing up, be careful not to say it in an *accusative* fashion. What makes the difference is your attitude, your heart, and your manner of speech. Don't say, "Dad, you never loved me." Say, "*I know you love me. And I love you. But I didn't always know that, and now I want to cause more love.*" Say it in a helpful way. Some people will still take it accusatively, but if you keep giving affection, they will know better.

You do not need to become a constant hugger if that is not your nature, but you should go to the limits of your normal means of expression, which is probably far more than your parents have been getting, and they do need it.

If you keep on giving affection after the questions you get back, you will soften your parents. In a matter of weeks, months, or years (the timeline varies with different people), you will see a real turnaround. Be patient, and keep on showing love.

There are two problems to take care of in your relationship with your parents—the heart problem and the action problem. The heart problem is first. Only a true heart repentance will 1) stop the curse, 2) cause long life, and 3) turn the three or four generations of bad news around to a thousand generations of good news. Your own unlove, your disrespect, and your ungratefulness towards your parents have to be taken care of in repentance toward God. To write these letters without being forgiven by God only ensures that your letters will be insincere and hypocritical. You may have a long wait if you wait for your father to turn to you first. You cannot afford the wait, so get right with God now. After you are clean, write the letters. Then continue writing, calling, texting, and visiting your parents, expressing respect, love, and thankfulness.

Doing these things will change you. You will become a better husband, son, and father, or a better wife, daughter, and mother. Your love and obedience will bring love for a thousand generations.

More Books by Jim Wilson

How to Be Free from Bitterness

When bitterness takes root in our hearts, its effects are anything but small. This collection of short articles discusses what it means to live as "imitators of God."

How to Be Free from Anxiety

This booklet teaches you how to trust God and be free from anxiety every day. God knows our needs, God is faithful, and He cares for you.

How to Maintain Joy in Your Life

This booklet helps us see how failure to confess sins steals our joy and how keeping short accounts—both with God and with others— sets us free to rejoice in the Lord no matter the circumstances.

Answered Prayer: The Faithfulness of God Made Manifest

Learn what the Bible teaches about prayer, study examples of answered prayer, and read Jim's personal stories from seven decades of walking with the Lord.

Principles of War: A Handbook on Strategic Evangelism

Not all warfare is waged on a battlefield: every Christian is called to be a soldier. This book outlines the fundamental principles of war and explains how we can employ them in our daily spiritual battles.

Contact Us

Community Christian Ministries

P.O. Box 9754

Moscow, ID 83843

Phone: (208) 883–0997

E-mail: ccm@moscow.com

Website: ccmbooks.org

To find out more about Community Christian Ministries, join our mailing list at ccmbooks.org or scan the QR code below.